Radical Recovery Workbook

Transforming the Despair of your Divorce into an Unexpected Good

Suzy Brown

Abilene, TX

Radical Recovery Workbook

Copyright 2007 by Suzy Brown

ISBN 978-0-89112-508-2

Printed in the United States of America

ALL RIGHTS RESERVED
No part of this publication may be reproduced, stored in a retrieval system, or transmitted in any form by any means—electronic, mechanical, photocopying, recording or otherwise—without prior written consent.

Scripture quotations, unless otherwise noted, are from The Holy Bible, New International Version. Copyright 1984, International Bible Society. Used by permission of Zondervan Publishers.

Cover design by Nicole Weaver
Interior design by Sandy Armstrong

For information contact:
Leafwood Publishers, Abilene, Texas
1-877-816-4455 toll free
www.leafwoodpublishers.com

07 08 09 10 11 12 / 7 6 5 4 3 2 1

Welcome to the *Radical Recovery* Workbook

I'm glad you're here, but I'm also sorry you're here. If you are reading the book and using this workbook, you are most likely experiencing the heartbreak of a midlife divorce. I wish I could put my arms around each one of you to comfort and encourage you and to tell you that everything will be all right. From where you are right now, you probably wouldn't believe me. Or you might be angry that I would even say that. Or you might be thinking, "Maybe life can sort of be okay at some point, but never really wonderful again." Remember—the strategies in the book and in this workbook come from women who have been where you are. We know how you're feeling. We understand your despair. We've been on the "dark side" of this experience, too.

It took me a long time to get to a place where I didn't ache every single day. The women in the first RADICAL group all suffered; but we also learned some things that can make your journey easier. I went through the ordeal kicking and sobbing and screaming. I want to save you some of the anguish I went through. I can't save you from all of it. Some of it you simply have to get through yourself, but I want you to know that your life can be good again. And not just ho-hum good. But unbelievably good. Extravagantly good. God can use this experience to bring you a new fulfillment, contentment, and joy that, from where you are now, you don't think is possible. I am here to tell you that it's not only possible … it's promised.

I know, too, that committing to anything right now is hard. Committing to a meeting once a week takes energy and effort that is mostly going into getting from one day to the next. But however weak you may be feeling, make the decision to survive. Make the decision to rise above this. Make the decision to trust God to bring something good out of it. You really have two choices: Be bitter and sad and angry the rest of your life; or figure out how to use this devastation to discover an amazing, unexpectedly joy-filled life.

This workbook was created to be used along with the *Radical Recovery* book. The workbook can be used as an individual study guide, or with one or two friends, or in a group setting. If you want to use it on your own, just go through the chapters at your own pace. As a group study, it is set up as a ten-week study that includes a one-week introduction, eight lessons, and a one-week conclusion. The benefits of doing this with a group is that you develop an invaluable support network of other women who are facing the same issues you are facing.

The women who met together at the very beginning of my divorce saga were wonderful women who all contributed to the concepts and strategies in this book. Each woman helped with the healing process. We shared ideas. We shared discouragements. We shared victories and insights. We laughed and cried. If possible, put together a group and see how much strength and encouragement you gain from each other. Ask other women going through midlife divorce to join you. We had a woman in our original group who had been divorced one day the first time she came to our meeting; we had another who had been divorced almost six years. The rest of us were somewhere in between. There are women out there who are struggling as you are. Develop your own group, start the study, and discover real and lasting goodness and joy and peace in your life. Use this situation to experience God in a deeper more intimate way. When you do that, love and laughter will find you again. Be patient. But know, without a shadow of a doubt, your life is about to blossom as never before.

RADICAL Meeting schedule

WEEK ONE: DATE_____ TIME_____

    Exchange names and information. Discuss meeting rules and boundaries. Discuss goals for the class. Share your personal starting point and what you want to get out of the class.

WEEK TWO: DATE_____ TIME_____

    First, Survive. Survival strategies for: Getting out of bed. Preparing to face the day. Choosing how to dress. Eating well. Nourishing your mind. Motivating yourself to get moving. Adjusting. Taking care of your own physical self. Being thankful.

WEEK THREE: DATE_____ TIME_____

    Get Strong. Setting physical goals. Staying balanced. Choosing your own power trip. Developing your new personal best. Dealing with alcohol. Confronting depression.
    Finding emotional and spiritual strength. Meditating and creating a breath prayer.

WEEK FOUR: DATE_____ TIME_____

    Organize the Chaos. De-cluttering—physically and emotionally. Getting your finances and important papers in order. Addressing personal safety and household maintenance. Maximizing those areas of life that you can control. Setting new personal goals.

WEEK FIVE: DATE_____ TIME_____

    Help Your Children. Listening to and guiding your children. Emphasizing positive lessons. Being honorable. Maintaining discipline and teaching responsibility. Having fun. Identifying your spiritual legacy. Giving your children the freedom to grow.

WEEK SIX: DATE_____TIME_____

    Stay Close to Family and Friends. Finding support. Staying positive. Maintaining connections. Telling people what you need. Fostering good relationships with acquaintances, community groups, support groups, the world at large.

WEEK SEVEN: DATE_____TIME_____

    Face Reality. Accepting where you are. Getting closure. Learning to be single. Dealing with difficult social situations. Getting to know your new best self. Discovering your desires, dreams, goals. Starting to see God's plan.

WEEK EIGHT: DATE_____TIME_____

    Choose to Change. Learning new self-talk. Choosing victory/not victimhood. Choosing the future you want. Dealing with emotions. Appreciating now. Rediscovering nature. Counting your blessings. Concentrating on spreading goodness wherever you can.

WEEK NINE: DATE_____TIME_____

    Embrace Transformation. Moving forward. Discovering the freedom of forgiveness. Taking control. Seeing the potential in your new life. Surrendering. Learning to be courageous. Being honest with God. Believing God's promises.

WEEK TEN: DATE_____TIME_____

    New Life. Trusting. Delighting. Committing. Giving up anger and fear. Finding new optimism. Experiencing new power. Accepting God's comfort. Being alert to those who need you. Blessing others. Review. Questions. Topics not covered. Final discussions.

Week 1

Who Are We?
And What Are We Doing Here?

1. Getting Acquainted

2. Class Boundaries

3. Goals for the Study

GETTING ACQUAINTED

Go around the room and give your name and tell how much or how little of your story you want to tell. Information should include your real name, your stage name (see below), children and ages, how long you have been divorced, and contact information: address, phone numbers, e-mail address. Fill out the information sheets on each woman in the class. Figuring out your stage name is easy. As explained in the introduction of the *Radical Recovery* book, this is an old recipe for deciding your stage name. I learned this from one of my book club friends. Your first name is the name of your first pet (or of your first doll if you didn't have a pet, or just pick a funky name you like). My dog's name was Frisky. Your last name is usually the name of the street where you lived in elementary school. I lived on Ridgewood Street. So my name became Frisky Ridgewood. If your street name doesn't work (like 52nd Street), pick a side street or just another street name you like. Actually, you can just pick out whatever name you want your stage name to be.

RADICAL RULES AND BOUNDARIES

Rule #1: Everything is Strictly Confidential

What is said or what happens in this room stays in this room. Period. This is a place where each of us can say what is in our heart regardless of how confused, angry, bitter, sad, distressing, or personal it is. We need to feel sure that what we say in these meetings is honest and an uncensored expression of what we are really feeling, and for that to happen we must be confident that the things we say will not be shared outside of this room. We should also listen to each other with the desire to understand and help, not to judge or put down. Accept each woman where she is on the journey. Share what you have learned or what you are struggling with. Be open. Be honest.

Rule # 2: No Alcohol

If this class is being run in a church or other similar setting, the "no alcohol" rule is accepted practice. Sometimes women who start their own neighborhood or area group think it would be okay to serve munchies and wine or other alcoholic beverages. That is not a good idea. It's okay for someone to be in charge of bringing goodies or for everyone to bring her own soft drink, coffee, apple cider, or whatever. Make the gathering as casual and as easy on everyone as possible. We are here to talk about our journey to recovery; we are not here to impress anyone with our cooking or hostess skills. We are definitely not here to sip wine and commiserate together about how sad our situation is. We are here to move forward.

Rule # 3: Find a Safe Meeting Place

Find a centrally located place to meet. We have found that it is usually best to have one central place and use that place for all ten meetings. There is less confusion that way and there is less frustration trying to find a new meeting place each week … for the organizer and for all of the participants. Make sure there are no distractions and that you choose a place where what you say is heard only by your group. If you are not meeting at a public place, find a house without family members or others present.

Rule #4: No New Members After the Second Meeting

This is not an absolutely hard and fast rule, but in general, it is best not to invite people to come into the gathering in the middle of the ten weeks. There are several reasons for this. For one thing, the lessons are meant to build on each other. They follow a certain progression of growth. The first lessons deal with survival … and we end up at the "Embrace Transformation" and "New Life" sections, which cannot be as helpful without the steps that precede them. Also, your group will develop a very close bond. You are sharing heartache and anguish as well as hope. That sharing brings you close in a way that is not possible in most other settings. A new person coming in halfway through the study might not feel the personal support as much as she could by starting at the beginning with a new group. However, as a group you will need to make these determinations yourself. Don't turn someone away who seems especially desperate (each of us?!) or who feels as if she can't wait for another group.

Goals for this study

1. Survive
2. Get strong
3. Get organized
4. Be a positive influence on:
    A. Our children
    B. Our extended family
    C. Our friends
    D. Our world
5. Discover God's purpose for our new life
6. Joyfully and passionately embrace this new life
7. Develop a new intimacy with God and with others
8. Share what we learn
9. Personal goals

Where are you now?

Think about how you are feeling now. Describe some of your thoughts in the space below. Be honest about this starting point. I know that most of the women in the first Radical Recovery group were feeling hopeless, alone, sad, afraid, worried, etc. Are those some of the things you are experiencing? What else?

Where do you want to be?

All of us desire to get back to joy. We want to feel confident again and desirable and excited about life. List and talk about some of the desires you have for the future.

Keep these in mind as you progress through the study.

 Week 2

Read the Welcome and Chapter One of *Radical Recovery*.

Fill in the answers to the questions below. Discuss at the next meeting.

First, Survive

RADICAL TRUTH

> "Fear not, for I am with you. Do not be dismayed.
> I am your God. I will strengthen you; I will help you;
> I will uphold you with my victorious right hand."
>
> Isaiah 41:10 (Living Bible)

What are the most pressing daily problems you are having? Eating? Sleeping? Doing simple daily tasks?

What is the hardest thing for you to adjust to?

Are you getting out of bed every day?

While you are still in bed, read the verse at the start of this week's study. Close your eyes and think about what it means. Remember that God gives you the power to face anything and everything. He will be with you every minute of this day. Ask for his help and he will give it. You can't always feel his help immediately, but he is working behind the scenes every single second.

List reasons to get out of bed. How do you think you'll feel if you don't?

What kind of message does staying in bed send your children if they are home?

A RADICAL Tip

Before you get out of bed every morning, starting with your head and neck, flex and release the muscle groups that move each part of your body. End with your toes. Be thankful for each part of your body. Repeat the verse at the start of this chapter.

Pray this simple prayer:

God help me today. You have promised to give me the strength to get through this day. You have promised that you won't allow anything to separate me from you. Help me show my children and those around me that I can make it through this day, and that I can joyfully, confidently shine your light as I do the things I need to do today.

Amen

Write down one way you can shine today.

Take A Shower

Go buy some special soap that you like. Go to a bath/spa/fragrance shop and pick out one bar of soap that you love. What kind is it? Write down why you like it. What color is it? How does it smell? Try to find something invigorating. Something with a punch that will wake you up and get your body revved up and ready to go! *Write down fresh, invigorating scents that you like.*

Remind yourself that your shower every morning is an amazing, unbelievable privilege. Ask God to help women all over the world who do not have this privilege. *While you are in the shower, think of five things that you are thankful for. Write them down.*

Get rid of five harmful negative thoughts or feelings this week. Write them down, get in the shower, wash them away and when you get out draw a line through them. If you have time write down a positive thought to replace each negative thought. For example write down the word "discouragement," then draw a line through it and in its place write "hope" or "optimism." If a negative thought or emotion pops up sometime during the day, just remember that you don't have to embrace that feeling, so visualize it washing away. Replace that negative emotion with a definite positive thought immediately.

Negative Thoughts	**Positive Thoughts**
1.	1.
2.	2.
3.	3.
4.	4.
5.	5.

RADICAL TRUTH

Think about this verse as you are getting dressed every morning:

"For God did not give us a spirit of timidity
but a spirit of power and love and self control."

2 Timothy 1:7 (RSV)

Say to yourself five times: "God is with me!" Think of today as the start of a stage of life that can be both good and God-directed. Write down how you can exhibit a sense of power and love and self-control today.

Fix Your Face

Think of five things you are thankful for right now. Go buy the book *14,000 Things To Be Happy About.* Read two pages every day. Start your own list of things to be happy about—the color yellow, frisky puppies, friends, a bowl of strawberries and real cream, clean sheets, black-capped chickadees, pictures on your refrigerator, your hands. Start a gratitude journal. *Get a notebook or use your daily planner and keep a running list of things you're thankful for. Start with five now.*

1.
2.
3.
4.
5.

A RADICAL Tip

SMILE! Go rent a really funny movie or get a video collection of "I Love Lucy" television shows or "The Best of Johnny Carson" or "The Andy Griffith Show." Try some other fun movie. Laughter is a proven antidote to all sorts of ills. God told us that through Solomon centuries ago. Science is proving it to be true.

Go get a facial at a spa or get a free makeup demonstration at a department store. Buy a new lipstick. Physically make yourself smile. Look out the window and smile. Look at a picture of your kids and smile. Look at a picture that one of your grandchildren drew for you and smile. Watch a bird or a squirrel and smile. *Write down five things you have smiled about or can smile about today.*

1.
2.
3.
4.
5.

Get Dressed

Really "get dressed" every day this week. Don't just throw on something. Actually put on something that makes you feel good about yourself. Even if you are just working around the house or working out or going to the grocery store, make the choice to put on something fun and comfortable but that still looks great. *Write down your favorite "relaxing" outfit. Why do you like it? How about your favorite "everyday" going-to-a-meeting outfit? Describe your favorite "dressy" outfit.*

Have your "colors" done. Go "shopping" (not necessarily buying). Ask a friend what colors look best on you. *What colors do you really enjoy wearing? Write them down in the space below.* Do you have anything in your closet in those colors? If you don't, make an effort to buy a piece of clothing in one of those colors.

A RADICAL Tip

Put on something bright and cheerful. You will feel better about yourself and you will look better to those around you if you take some care in choosing what you wear. Our feelings often follow our actions, so take the action to look as good as you can. You can still be comfortable and you don't have to "dress up" all the time, but dress like you want to feel. Remember to smile! Even if you have to fake it occasionally.

Make yourself put on that piece of jewelry you love. In fact, go buy a silver bracelet or a ring or a pendant. It doesn't have to be expensive. (In fact, it can be really inexpensive!) Every time you look at your bracelet or ring or necklace, say to yourself, "I am a wonderful, worthy, warrior woman. I will use this situation to become more beautiful and joyful than I have ever been." Have "RADICAL" engraved on the inside or just write it in you daily planner every day this week. *Write "I am a RADICAL woman" five times below.* Remember what those words mean.

RADICAL TRUTH

> "Therefore, as God's chosen people, holy and dearly loved, clothe yourselves with compassion, kindness, humility, gentleness and patience. ... And over all these virtues put on love, which binds them all together in perfect unity."
>
> Colossians 12;14 (NIV)
>
>

What does this verse above mean to you in your situation? Explain.

Remember that who you are on the inside is more important than how you look on the outside. Make sure you are dressed with right living. And remember that right living brings its own joyful rewards. Even though you feel as if your right living brought nothing but despair, just keep on doing right and the joy will come, the gladness will come, even the fun will come. Write down five "right" things you can do this week.

Eat Something

Pretend you are at a health spa. Go to the grocery store and pick out things that are beautiful to look at and healthy to eat. A beautiful shiny eggplant. Strawberries. Blueberries. Carrots. Radishes. Apples. Kiwi. Dark green veggies contain lots of the nutrients we need. Spinach, broccoli, and brussell sprouts are good along with tomatoes, green beans, tangerines, cantaloupe, apricots and raspberries. Thank God for the glorious blessing of going to the store and picking out wonderful things to eat. Pray for all the women in the world who don't have enough to eat. Send a donation somewhere for people who are hungry. *Write down your five favorite veggies and your five favorite fruits.* Buy some the next time you go to the store and be thankful you have the ability to do that.

HEALTHY TIPS

> When you buy breads, buy whole grains. Crackers, breads, cereal are all more nutritious if they are made with whole grain. Make sure "whole wheat" or "whole grain," is the first item listed on the list of ingredients.
>
> Eat healthy snacks. Dried fruit; nuts; carrot sticks; pretzels; celery; a hard-boiled egg (and while you're at it, buy eggs from local farms if they

are available. Buy eggs from "happy hens" (i.e. free-range chickens who get to roam around). I buy eggs at my local grocery store from an Amish farm. They often put a little note in each egg carton about something that is going on at the farm! Here is the message from the carton of eggs I bought today. (Start appreciating even the little things like this note that connects you to other people.) "Farmers Luck—What is it? Is it when things go wrong day after day—the beans aren't filled, the hens don't lay. The cow is dry, oh me-oh my! Or is it when the sun is bright and everything seems to be alright—the hens are laying hundred fold. The corn is tall and bright as gold. Ho-hum—Ho hum, don't you think we need the two—to keep us happy, humble and true.—Stanberry Community Farms."

Keep a food journal for one week and see what and how much you are actually eating. Most of us eat too much or we eat when we are not hungry. During this period of time, you might not be eating enough, so monitor for one week what you eat. Keep track of everything you put in your mouth for one whole week. That will give you a good idea as to whether you are getting enough of the famous four food groups. If you are trying to lose weight, it's been shown that people who record what they are eating keep their calorie intake lower than those who don't keep track.

Most of the time it's best to really savor and pay attention to what you are eating. Occasionally in your particular situation, an encouraging diversion is all right. It's okay to read something worthwhile or fun while you eat. Find a good book about some topic that interests you and read a chapter at lunch. Read through the New Testament a chapter or two at a time at breakfast. Read a joke book for jokes that you can share with your grandchildren. *List below three topics you might like to explore.*

Invite a friend over for breakfast, lunch, or dinner. If you don't feel like cooking, stop by the deli and get something you will enjoy and eat it out on the deck. If no one is available to join you, re-read one of your favorite childhood books (or even watch a good TV show) while you eat. Invigorate your mind as you nourish your body. *What was your favorite childhood book? Why did you like it? Does it mean anything in your situation now?*

GET MOVING

Do little things every day to keep your body moving. Simple things like raising your arms over your head and taking a deep breath. Stretch. Right now and at least once every day this week, just stand up and move your head in a circle. Shrug your shoulders. Touch the floor. Be aware of your body and how amazing and wonderful it is. Stand up, lift your arms and take a deep breath. Stretch on tiptoe. Say, "Thank you God for this body!" (Whatever shape it's in). *Name five parts of your body that you are especially grateful for and why.*

Try a motivational tape that encourages you to get moving. Get a tape with workout music. Have one of your children or grandchildren make you a tape with great, upbeat songs. Listen to it and be thankful you are alive. You still have so many good things in your life. God can use this experience to transform you. Discover a new genre of music. *List some kinds of music you especially enjoy.*

Get dressed and go out the door today and go someplace! Take your newspaper and daily planner and go to a comfortable coffee place. Go to the gym and workout. Call a friend and walk briskly for twenty minutes. Get moving to work. Be thankful for your job. As you are driving or riding to work, pray that God will direct you to people who need you today. Be a giver. Forget about your trauma whenever you can today. I know (especially at the beginning) how hard that is. But be the absolute best employee you can be today.

Be the best volunteer. Be the most enthusiastic gardener or organizer you can be today. *Write below a prayer of thanksgiving that today you have the ability to move. Thank God that you can choose to move and that you have the freedom to go where you want to go today. Include in your prayer a request for encouragement for those people who are bedridden or paralyzed or who do not have the freedom to move as you do.* Rent and watch the movie "Emmanuel's Gift." Be thankful and inspired. Google the words "physical disabilities," and see what comes up. Pick one, do a little research and send in a small donation. Sign up to Bike for Diabetes or Walk for Heart or whatever. Your body is the temple of God's Spirit. Be thankful for it and use it for the good of others.

Discuss any other issues from these first two chapters in the book. Discuss issues that have bothered you this last week. Talk about solutions.

Week Three

Read Chapter Two in
Radical Recovery.

Fill out the questions below and discuss at your next meeting

GET STRONG

RADICAL TRUTH

> "It is God who arms me with strength
> and makes my way perfect."
>
> Psalm 18:32 (NIV)

Name a strong woman you have known in your life.

What characteristics does she have?

Has she had any obstacles to overcome? What were they? How did she deal with them?

Did you ever see her cry? Or discouraged? If so does that mean she is weak? *Explain.*

RADICAL TRUTH

> **Think about this verse this week:**
>
> "Glory and honor are in his presence; strength and gladness are in his place."
>
> 1 Chronicles 16:27 (KJV).
>
>

Put that verse in your own words. What does it mean to you today?

List some ways you can begin to "get strong" physically?

Keep a RADICAL workout diary. Do 20-30 minutes of weight training three days a week and 20-30 minutes of aerobic work (walking, running, biking) three days a week. *Set a fitness goal. Write it down in the space below.* Be specific. Make it a priority to work up a sweat and get yourself in shape. Record what you do to reach your goal every day for this week. Put a picture of someone who looks physically fit (not some ridiculously skinny model who survives on grapefruit and mineral water, but a real person) on your refrigerator. Imagine yourself with the body and strength you want. Go get some hand weights at the sporting goods store. Or use cans from your pantry.

Walk as often as you can this week. Walk somewhere once a day. Walk strong! Don't shuffle along. If you are walking around the block or for your aerobic exercise, even if you are crying, feel the cleansing. Be bold. Don't be embarrassed if you cry. Pray as you walk. Pray specifically for the people you love. Pray for your children. Pray for your family. Pray for your ex-husband. Thank God for his blessings. Chant something uplifting as you walk. Say the words in time with your steps. How about something like "God is blessing me every day in every way." Or "I am strong and good." Get some powerful personal chant in your head. Believe it. *Write your chant below.*

A RADICAL Tip

You have the power to get in shape. Do it! Work at it! Don't be a wimp! Commit to doing what it takes to get your body in shape. Everything else will go better. You will feel better. You will sleep better. Just remember that you are the temple of God. Don't abuse or mistreat or take for granted your personal temple of the Holy Spirit. Set a goal for how you want your body to look one year from now and start working little by little, but diligently toward that goal. Find a workout partner. Be accountable to your journal, to your partner, and to yourself! As Nike says, "Just Do It!"

Go buy some women's multivitamins and start taking them.

Remember to keep your food diary. Use this life experience to fine-tune your eating habits. Use this time to become a healthier you. I know food may not sound good right now, but decide to become a more vigorous, more vital you. Eat five **small** meals a day. Go to the store and stock up on healthy, easy to fix, easy to eat foods. If you have kids at home, buy some comfort foods … don't feel guilty. Don't overeat, but enjoy. *Write down your reasons for treating your body with respect.*

Eat foods that will make you strong! You are a Warrior Woman ... a RADICAL Woman. Cut back on stuff that will make you flabby and fat and listless. *Write down five foods you eat but that have little food value.* Stop eating those things every day from boredom or for comfort. You can eat them on Sunday or whatever day you decide to be your "free" day. Skip them on the other days.

Drink at least 6-8 glasses of water a day. Put a checkmark for every glass of water you drink at the corner of every page in your daily planner. Are there 6-8 checkmarks on most days? You know it's good for you. Do it. Find the most special glass in your house. Use that as your own personal water glass (Go get a new one if you want). Make this your 8-glassfuls of water glass. *Describe your glass below.*

Are you drinking alcohol? Are you keeping your drinking well within moderation parameters? How much are you drinking every week? Be honest.

Are you dealing with your depression? Have you talked with your counselor or physician about antidepressants? Physical exercise and maintaining some control of your life have both been proven to help combat depression. Keep doing what you can, but ask for help if you need it. *Explain how you personally feel about taking antidepressants.*

Getting Strong Spiritually

RADICAL TRUTH

> "Exercise daily in God—no spiritual flabbiness, please! Workouts in the gymnasium are useful, but a disciplined life in God is far more so, making you fit both today and forever."
>
> 1 Timothy 4:7b-8 (The Message)

Make a commitment to spend time in prayer, meditation and study of the scripture every day this week. Keep a prayer diary or use your daily planner. Write down your prayers. Leave space for God's answers. Get real with God. Tell him exactly what you are feeling and thinking. Tell him what you are mad about. Tell him what you are sad about. Tell him what you want. What your hopes are. Thank him for all of your unbelievable blessings. Thank him for what he is doing in your life right now even though you might not understand it. *Write a personal prayer below.* Say what you are really feeling, not what you think you should be feeling. God knows your heart anyway, so be honest.

A RADICAL Tip

Get a paperback copy of the New Testament translation called "The Message." Write with bold marker on the cover of the book: "God's RADICAL [MESSAGE] to (your stage name—or your real name)" and read a chapter every day. Underline in different colors. Put stars by the parts that speak specifically to you. Drink in the words and the ideas. Pay attention to the promises. Pick out a verse from your reading, write it down on an index card and keep it with you all day. Write it at the top of the page for the day in your daily planner. Read it whenever you think about it. Every morning surrender to God's will for you for this one day.

Practice meditating on God and his love and goodness. Sit quietly. Close your eyes. Say something about God to yourself that is meaningful to you. I like the words, "God is in control." Or "God's promises are sure." Or "God's will is perfect." Focus on one phrase for three minutes. Set the timer. Increase the time as you get better at this. *Write your God truth below.*

Pick a breath prayer for this week. A breath prayer is a short, two part prayer that you can say in one breath. One part on the inhale, one part on the exhale. Example: "Thank you God (as you inhale) … for loving me," (as you exhale). Or "Holy God (as you inhale) … shine through me," (as you exhale). Every time you are worried, or you have a distressing thought, or just anytime during the day, consciously take a breath and repeat your breath prayer. *Write your own breath prayer below.* Use it this week.

Discuss any issues that are still unresolved from this week's study.

Week Four

Read Chapter Three in *Radical Recovery*.

Fill out the questions below and discuss at your next meeting.

ORGANIZE THE CHAOS

RADICAL TRUTH

> "God does not lead us into a disorderly, unkempt life but into something holy and beautiful—as beautiful on the inside as the outside."
>
> 1 Thessalonians 4:7 (The Message)

In what ways are you beautiful on the inside? Are these characteristics being shown in your actions? *Explain.*

Make a list of some of the emotional junk that is cluttering up your mind right now. Think about ways to get rid of the not so beautiful things like bitterness, rage, fear and other negative emotions. Can you replace these negative thoughts with something positive? Explain below.

Declutter your personal space! Go through your house room by room and make an effort to get rid of anything that you do not love or do not use. Get rid of broken things you are going to fix "someday." Pretend you are on the show "What NOT to Wear." Get rid of clothes that don't fit or you don't like for whatever reason. Give away things. Throw away things. This is a new life. You need mental and physical space to grow and shine. *Make a list of things you can get rid of.* Be bold.

A RADICAL Tip

Get rid of all those knick-knacks that you have sitting around that may no longer have any meaning to you. Clean up your living space. Clear out your work space. By having your environment clutter free you have space for new ideas in your life and for new opportunities. Also, by having your environment clutter free, you are less distracted. A midlife divorce is stressful, and your mind is spinning in a thousand directions. You forget things. You lose things. You misplace things. You forget appointments. By having your space less cluttered, you have a better chance to stay focused and you have fewer distractions.

Is there anything physical that you have had to give up that still hurts you to think about? Is there anything you can do about that loss that would make it easier to deal with? *Brainstorm below.*

What are some of the things that you might have to get now that you are a single woman that you didn't need to worry about when you were married?

Get some sort of daily planner. It can be as simple or as intricate as you want. I used a big 8 ½" x 11" Franklin Covey planner with two full pages for each day. I also made use of their exercise pages and their pages to keep track of important numbers, financial information, food diaries, household inventories, etc. Find a planner that you like and use it. *Write below some of the things you need to keep track of now.*

Figure out what to do with the family pictures, the holiday stuff, and other personal items. If nothing else, buy some storage tubs and label them and put these undecided things away until you feel strong enough to deal with them. That may be next month, next year or maybe never. Box them up, and if you can't get rid of them yet, at least get those sad reminders out of your immediate space. Get them out of your face for the time being. Don't feel as if you have to tackle everything all at once. I still haven't dealt with the pictures, and my divorce was over six years ago. *List below a few of the distressing, hard-to-confront items that you need to get out of your day-to-day space.*

Do you know where you stand financially? If not, do you have a plan to figure out where you are and where you want to be and how you are going to get there? How do you plan to get this piece of your life under control? *Explain.*

RADICAL TRUTH

> **Is giving part of your financial plan?**
> **Do you believe the following verses from the Bible?**
>
> "Give, and it will be given to you. A good measure, pressed down, shaken together and running over, will be poured into your lap. For with the measure you give, it will be measured to you."
>
> Luke 6:38 (NIV)
>
> **And**
>
> "Remember this: Whoever sows sparingly will also reap sparingly, and whoever sows generously will also reap generously. Each man should give what he has decided in his heart to give, not reluctantly or under compulsion, for God loves a cheerful giver. And God is able to make all grace abound to you, so that in all things at all times, having all that you need, you will abound in every good work."
>
> 2 Corinthians 9:6-9 (NIV)
>
>

Are you willing to try God's plan to financial peace? *Explain how you might start doing that?*

Set aside some time every day to get your paperwork in order. Make sure you have all of the important documents you need. Get a filing system in place. Go get a file box or some big expandable files from your favorite office supply place. I have a red one for my bills and expenses, and a green one for my work bills, expenses, and receipts. Some people like household files, personal files, family files, medical files. At this time, the less complicated the better. The fewer the decisions you have to make the better. Your life right now is a mass of big, huge decisions, so make the little, daily decisions as easy as possible. *List below the papers you need to keep track of on an ongoing basis.*

Set up a bill-paying center or set up your computer to pay bills on line. Get some help if you need it. My very organized daughter set up a bill-paying center for me. It included everything I need to pay bills. *Make a list of what you need in your bill-paying center.* Make sure you have those things on hand.

Also set aside a few minutes every week (I try to do this on Sunday afternoon) to send a note to someone you care about. It is a wonderful treat to receive a handwritten, "I'm glad you're in my life" note in the mail. During the week I also try to cut out articles that I know might be of help or interest to someone I know, and then put that article in an envelope with a note. People appreciate your care. *Make a list below of what you need in your personal correspondence, letter-writing center and a few people you would like to encourage.*

After your decluttering process, go through your house and make an inventory and take pictures of your belongings. List valuables (artwork, silver, china, crystal, furniture) and give them a monetary value. Some insurance companies encourage photos of your home furnishings. This will help greatly if something should happen to your house and things need to be replaced.

Go through your house or apartment and make sure it is safe and secure. Most local police departments will go through your home with you and check for safety and security hazards. Follow their advice. If your windows and doors are not secure, hire someone or have a friend or neighbor help get them up to safety par. Change your locks if you need to. *List safety concerns below.* Ask the police what you can do about them.

NECESSARY MAINTENANCE

Set up schedules for regular home maintenance. Write the dates here or in your daily planner.

Make these appointments for yourself:
- Get your teeth cleaned and checked
- Get a physical
- Get a mammogram and a pap smear
- Get a colonoscopy if you need one
- Have a bone densitometry measurement

Make these appointments for your car:
- Oil change
- Brake check
- Air conditioner/heater check
- Windshield washer-fluid check
- Wiper blade replacement

Make these appointments for your home:
- Air conditioner/furnace check
- Gutters
- Pest control
- Others?

Can you start feeling more in control by setting some personal goals for this year? *List five things you want to accomplish in the next year. Include a physical goal, a spiritual goal, a financial goal, a family goal, and a personal goal.* By visualizing your goals, you can start to incorporate into your daily life actions that will help you reach those goals. Be bold. Don't hold back. You have a clean slate … take advantage of the potential in where you are today. Start taking control of your life now.

Discuss anything from this section that is still unresolved for you.

WEEK FIVE

Read Chapter Four in
Radical Recovery.

Fill out the questions below and discuss at your next meeting.

HELP YOUR CHILDREN

RADICAL TRUTH

> "God-loyal people, living honest lives, make it much easier for their children."
>
> Proverbs 20:7 (The Message)

How are your children doing? What seems to be the biggest adjustment they are having to make?

What do you want your ultimate spiritual statement to be to your children through all of this? *Write it down and read it over every day until it is in the forefront of your thoughts. It will make your decisions easier as you deal with daily frustrations and problems.*

Write down three positive things that your children can learn from this experience:

Be the same caring, concerned, dependable mother that you have always been for your children. Remember, you are the mother. They can't fix this for you. They are not here to prop you up. If your children are like my children, they were very patient and supportive, because I was a mess especially at first. But don't let that get out of hand. They know you are suffering. You would be a cold, dead fish if you weren't. Just do the best you can and make sure you are not making your children your support group. *List a few of the ways you can reassure your children that you are there for them.*

Even being civil to your ex-husband is sometimes difficult during this time, but maintain a solid sense of integrity and honorable actions as much as you possibly can. Is there any way you can help your children maintain a positive relationship with their father?

Are there things you are doing either consciously or unconsciously that make them feel guilty or uneasy about spending time with their father? *List those things below.*

I believe older children have a right to know the basics of why you are getting a divorce. Be as honest and straightforward as you can, but keep negative comments about your ex-husband to a minimum. Are there things you have said or done that you need to apologize to your children for or ask forgiveness for? *List them below and then take the appropriate corrective actions.* Give your children the blessing of freedom to deal with their father in the way they need to.

RADICAL TRUTH

> "Discipline your children while you have the chance; indulging them destroys them."
>
> Proverbs 19:18 (The Message)

Are you maintaining consistent discipline? Determine to stay on track. Praise the appropriate behavior of your children and correct them when they are not acting responsibly. *If you are having difficulty with discipline, list ways to improve your consistency.*

One of the most important things our children can learn from this is that choices have consequences. Are you letting your children take ever-increasing responsibility for their actions? Is that harder now? *Explain below.*

Think of one fun thing you can do with your children this week. *Write it down and make arrangements for that to happen.* Try to rediscover joy and keep an upbeat spirit even through this. Ask for God's help.

RADICAL TRUTH

> "Live a happy life! Keep your eyes open for GOD;
> watch for his works. Be alert for signs of his presence."
>
> Psalm 105:3-4 (The Message)
>
>

This week ask your children what they need most from you right now. *Write what you think their answers might be in the space below.* Compare what you have written to what they actually tell you.

Based on what your children have told you, *list some specific steps you can take to help them through this in a better way.*

Make sure your children have someone they can turn to (besides your ex-husband or yourself) if they need an objective opinion or just some other trustworthy person to talk with. *Write their names below.* If you need to, make an appointment for your child with a family counselor, a mentor at church, a wise family member or friend, or some other person you trust.

Think about new ways to do things in your family: *List a few family traditions that will need to be adjusted or changed.* Don't try to pretend things haven't changed.

A RADICAL Tip

Start a dialog about some new traditions. Think through a few ideas yourself first. Then get some ideas from your children. Do a little research about alternate ways of celebrating the holidays. The first Thanksgiving after our divorce, I took all of our children and spouses to an old restaurant known for its delicious seafood. We ate an early dinner then went to a totally crazy movie, "Being John Malcovitch." We changed everything for that one memory-filled holiday. We have since gone back to our more traditional celebration of that day with family and all the fixings. We have also considered going to a soup kitchen or homeless shelter to help for the day. However, we discovered that lots of people seem to volunteer on Thanksgiving and Christmas, so if that's what you decide to do, call ahead and "make reservations" for your family to do that early enough. Help put together and deliver holiday baskets at your church or call the Salvation Army and get the name of a family to help. Make helping others part of your new tradition.

List your child's teachers that you may want to tell about the situation. Perhaps only those closest to your child may need to know. Coaches. Favorite teachers. The counselor. The youth minister at church. Parents of close friends. Think of what you are going to say beforehand. These people don't need to know all of the ugly details, just enough information to make things easier for your children.

Discuss any unresolved issues from this week's study.

WEEK SIX

Read Chapter Five in *Radical Recovery.*

Answer the questions below and discuss at the next meeting.

STAY CLOSE TO FAMILY AND FRIENDS

Extended family

Try your best to continue extended family get-togethers. Be sure to tell your family how much you need their encouragement and support. Let them help you maintain connections. Encourage them to take an active part in reassuring your children through this situation. *List some specific ways they can help.* Call them this week and tell them what you need or e-mail them your list and specifically ask for their help.

Contact your ex-husband's family and, if appropriate, let them know you are interested in maintaining a relationship. Reassure grandparents that they will still have an opportunity for a relationship with their grandchildren. Foster that relationship if you can. Talk to your children about both extended families and let them take the lead, but encourage them to keep in touch. *List a few ways you can help them do this.*

RADICAL TRUTH

> "Just as lotions and fragrance give sensual delight,
> a sweet friendship refreshes the soul."
>
> Proverbs 27:9 (The Message)

Recently I read the account of a man in training for the Navy Seals. One of the things that kept him going when he didn't want to, or felt as if he couldn't, was his connection with and commitment to others in his group who were going through the same thing. Use the friends in your group or find another friend who has had a similar experience and encourage each other. Cry together. Vent together. Don't try to do this all by yourself. Develop a support group and use it for … SUPPORT. It is not a group you meet with once a week and then forget about. Help each other. Pray for each other. *What support do you need most right now? Explain below.*

List three people you can call if you are feeling especially sad or lonely or angry or frustrated. Write their names and phone numbers or e-mail addresses where you can keep them with you all the time. Call them **when** (not if) you need to. Don't suffer alone. This is not the time to win the Miss Independence award!

A RADICAL Tip

Call a friend and tell her you just need to go have a little fun. Go bowling or to a funny movie or just order pizza and hang out. Be clear about what you need. From personal experience, I went to a movie "just for fun" with a friend and ended up crying in the car afterwards because the movie turned out to be a light drama-comedy in which a couple broke up and then got back together at the end of the movie. In spite of the temporary sobbing, it still turned out to be a wonderful evening. Just learn to expect the unexpected and let yourself be emotional however you need to be. Your friends will understand, and this stage won't last forever.

RADICAL TRUTH

> Remember the verse: "Finally brothers, whatever is true, whatever is noble, whatever is right, whatever is pure, whatever is lovely, whatever is admirable—if anything is excellent or praiseworthy—think about such things."
>
> Philippians 4:8 (NIV)

Make a list of five good, happy, uplifting things you can talk about with friends. See verse above.

Write out an answer for people you meet in the grocery store or at the post office who want to know what's going on. Word usually travels fast and people want to know how you are doing, or casual acquaintances may just be curious about what they have heard about your divorce. Frame the divorce in a way that maintains your integrity and your belief that, even though you may be struggling now, that you plan on learning and growing from this experience.

RADICAL TRUTH

> "Like a cool drink of water when you're worn out and weary is a letter from a long-lost friend."
>
> Proverbs 25:25 (The Message)

Reconnect with a good friend you have lost track of. I reconnected with my best friend from high school during this upheaval and spent a wonderful weekend with her, and we have been in contact ever since. *List three friends below with whom you might want to reconnect.* Find out how to get in touch with them, and then contact them.

List connections that you fear you might be losing. Is there anything you can do to prevent that, or are you going to choose to let some connections go to make room for new, more promising, less complicated relationships?

List connections that you think you will be able to maintain and foster.

A RADICAL Tip

If you are invited to a friend's house to a party, offer to come early and help in the preparations. Be positive and be there to serve. Don't expect sympathy or encouragement while they are getting ready for the party. Get your mind completely on helping, and in the process your evening might begin less awkwardly than if you came into the party alone.

YOUR COMMUNITY

Remember, it is *your* community. You are already a part of it whether you realize that or not. Be an active part. Contribute. *List three ideas of how you can be a helping hand to a group in your community.* Church. Non-profit groups. Nursing homes. Whatever philanthropic or political group you want to contribute time and energy to, do it. It will give you something to do; you will meet new people; and you will get your mind off of yourself.

What attractions in your community can you take advantage of? Bike trails? Art galleries? Museums? Your neighborhood symphony group? *List them below.* Get information about venues in your city that are of interest and get reacquainted. Pretend you are someone from another state or even another country and that you are here to find the unique specialties of your town. Uncover fun out-of-the way places where you can eat or visit. Explore. Step out of your comfort zone. *List your new discoveries.*

Support Group

If you are doing this study, you may already have a support group. If you are doing it on your own, try to find at least one or two other people to interact with on a deeply personal level. You are in the middle of a life-changing, stressful situation and you will find comfort and strength and even fun with other people who understand what you are going through. Don't stay with a group that you feel is not helping. Some groups are just not a good fit and that is the last thing you need at this point. However, if you can find one good contact within a group, it might be worth your time and energy to stay with the group and develop that relationship. Be patient, but if the group is not helping you move to a place you want to be, politely drop out.

A RADICAL Tip

In the beginning especially, don't go to a mixed support group with the hope of "finding someone." You need to get strong and center yourself first. You need to heal and regroup on your own before you even think about finding someone else. I think you can be more honest and straightforward in a group of women than in a mixed group. That's just my opinion. Women seem to have a few issues that are completely different than those confronted by men in this situation.

Discuss any unresolved issues about friends, your community, support groups.

Week Seven

Read Chapter Six in
Radical Recovery.

Answer the questions below and discuss at your next meeting.

Face Reality

RADICAL TRUTH

> "For I know the plans I have for you, declares the Lord,
> plans to prosper you and not to harm you,
> plans to give you hope and a future."
> Then you will call upon me and come and pray to me,
> and I will listen to you. You will seek me and find me
> when you seek me with all your heart."
>
> Jeremiah 29:11-13 (NIV)

Have you fully accepted the fact that you really are divorced? Are you beginning to see yourself as a single woman, not just a divorced woman? Think of yourself as a woman for whom God has a specific plan for hope and joy and an exciting, fulfilling future. *How does that thought change your attitude about your life now?*

In what ways would it be easier if your husband had died?

What have you done with your wedding ring? Your wedding pictures? Can you think of any ways that you might be able to get more closure?

How can you start answering the question, "Who am I now, today?"

List all of your roles right this minute.

Who do you want to be for yourself? If you had no connections to anyone this minute, how would you like for your life to unfold? *Name two goals you would embrace if the only person you had to think about was yourself.* Can you incorporate those goals into your life in any way now?

Do you see any positives about being single? *List them below.* The good things are hard to see right now, but try again!

List what you are being forced to learn about yourself.

Is this experience making you depend on God at a deeper level? If you don't have a relationship with God, can you use this experience to start the search for a spiritual base? Do you feel as if you can begin a relationship or create a deeper relationship with God?

List some ways that you might be able to do that.

RADICAL TRUTH

> "God has given each of you some special abilities;
> be sure to use them to help each other,
> passing on to others God's many kinds of blessings."
>
> I Peter 4:10 (Living Bible)

List five things you are good at:

Make a list of your desires. Think about your dreams, your goals, your passions.

List five things you really enjoy doing.

Start visualizing what you want your new life to look like. Write what you see.

Write down something good about yourself. Write down a new positive attribute every day this week. Concentrate on those good things when you feel tense or defeated about your new life. Each day concentrate on one power-filled strength you have written down about yourself. When you feel sad or worried, think about the fact that God made you exactly who you are, and that he wants to bless you and fill you with everything good. Believe him. Let him do it.

Discuss any issues from the Face Reality chapter that you still need to talk about.

Week Eight

Read Chapter Seven of *Radical Recovery.*

Answer the questions below and discuss at your next meeting.

CHOOSE TO CHANGE

RADICAL TRUTH

> "Be careful what you think. Your life is shaped by your thoughts."
>
> Proverbs 4:23 (Today's English Version)

Right now, how are you thinking and talking to yourself about this situation? *Describe.*

Explain below how are you talking to others about your situation.

Explain why it's better to see yourself as victorious rather than as a victim.

Who makes the decisions about how your life will be in the future? Who is in control of whether your life is joyful and exciting or full of mediocrity or despair?

RADICAL TRUTH

> "Make a careful exploration of who you are and the work you have been given, and then sink yourself into that. Don't be impressed with yourself. Don't compare yourself with others. Each of you must take responsibility for doing the creative best you can with your own life."
>
> Galatians 6:3-4 (The Message)

Does it help anything to think about how your life compares to your ex-husband's life? Or to concentrate on all the things he has that you don't? Or to think about what he and his girlfriend or new wife are doing? How can you turn off those thoughts? *Describe.*

What choices do you have today? Can you choose to be joyful instead of sad? To be courageous instead of defeated? To be strong instead of being pushed around by the actions of others and circumstances of life? *Make a list of a few positive choices you can make right now.*

How does your attitude affect the way you embrace life? *Explain.*

How are you dealing with the things that still upset you about this divorce? Do you have a strategy for dealing with anger? With sadness? With hurt? *Write down ways to deal with each of those three things.*

According to some experts, anger is valuable because it lets you know that a boundary has been violated. Fear lets you know that you need to prepare for some challenge. Hurt lets you know that an expectation has not been met. Can you use your anger, worry and hurt to change things for the better? What are you still angry about? What are you still sad about? How can you use these signals for positive change?

A RADICAL Tip

What good does it do to focus on how terrible this all is? In boot camp, does it help to cry and moan about how hard the training is? Can you get through it any faster when you complain and whine? You have to grieve. We know that. You have to mourn your losses, and it's a terrible, traumatic adjustment. Don't try to sidestep or hurry that process. Experience it. Then you are going to have to figure out how to get beyond it. Doing these exercises may be ahead of where you really are. But just having the discipline to do them can reassure you that you are at least moving in the right direction. Be patient. This process takes time. Just do the best you can wherever you are and keep your eyes forward as much as you can.

Does rage help anything for anyone? Does rage mean that you may still be fighting the reality of where you are now? *List three specific things you can do to more fully accept your new life situation.*

Learn to start "getting in the moment." *Make a list of every physical sensation you are experiencing right this moment.* What do you hear, feel, see, smell, taste?

Write down the only moment you have any control over.

A RADICAL Tip

Put the past in the past where it belongs. You cannot do one thing about what has already happened. Get fully into your life now.

Count your blessings of this moment. *Make a list of ten things you are thankful for this very moment.*

Start thinking about ways you can help other people. Contribute your talents and abilities to help or bring joy to someone else. Plan something special for your grandchildren. Do something nice for a friend. Help at church. Invite an older, single neighbor to share dinner with you. Use your suffering to help you be more aware of what other people might be going through. Make your own list below of some ways to brighten the day for someone else.

> ### A RADICAL Tip
>
> Take a walk outside if the weather allows it. Even if it's rainy or cold, dress for the weather and get outside. Take deep, full breaths. Put your head back, put your arms up and say, "Thank you!" Appreciate the fact that you live in a free country, and you are alive and you have a chance to make your life what you want it to be from this day on.

Put a picture of some inspiring scene on your computer screensaver. Have one of your children, grandchildren, nieces or nephews or a neighbor do it for you if you can't figure it out. Listen to a CD of nature sounds when you go to bed. There are CDs with the sounds of a prairie, an ocean, a mountain stream. Find a sound that brings you a feeling of peace. Write something below about your favorite time of day or your favorite natural environment. What do you most closely identify with? The forest? The beach? A meadow of wildflowers? A thunderstorm? Dawn?

Think about something positive in this moment and try to uncover even a tiny growing anticipation about good things to come. Be content in this one moment. God is working. Even though you might not be able to feel it fully right now, remember that the seeds of new growth are sprouting. A new flower is in bud and about to bloom. Describe below one good thing that might come from your divorce experience.

Discuss any unresolved issues from the Choose to Change chapter.

WEEK NINE

Read Chapter Eight in *Radical Recovery.*

Answer the questions below and discuss at your next meeting.

EMBRACE TRANSFORMATION

RADICAL TRUTH

> "God is kind, but He's not soft.
> In kindness, He takes us by the hand and
> leads us to a radical life change."
>
> Romans 2:4 (The Message)

What radical change do you want in your life?

Is that a change that will improve your life and move you forward from where you are right now?

Is there any way you can help get that change started immediately?

Have you forgiven your husband or ex-husband?

If not, what are you gaining by being unforgiving?

What is holding you back from forgiving him and letting go of the bitterness that unforgiveness causes?

What benefits can you name that will come from taking control of your life?

Where are you in your spiritual walk right now?

Can you take that radical step to believe that there is a master plan for your life that is unbelievably wonderful?

Are you able to see any of the potential of your new and better life now? Emotionally? Physically? Spiritually? *Explain.*

How do you feel about the idea of a God who knows you better than anyone and loves you more than you can even imagine?

RADICAL TRUTH

> **What do you think about the verse,**
>
> "And we know that all that happens to us is working for our good if we love God and are fitting into his plans"?
>
> Romans 8:28 (The Living Bible)
>
>

Can you think of any of God's purposes for you? Do you think those purposes might include some fun, some wildly extravagantly good things? What gives you that hope?

Can you truthfully say to God, "I surrender to your plans for me"? How does that make you feel? Explain below. Put your talents, abilities, dreams and hopes into God's hands. Are you going to let someone else's bad behavior destroy your life? Do you think God will forget his promises to you?

RADICAL TRUTH

> "... the Lord who created you ... says, 'Don't be afraid, for I have ransomed you; I have called you by name; you are mine. When you go through deep waters and great trouble I will be with you ...' 'All who claim me as their God will come, for I have made them for my glory.'"
>
> Isaiah 43:1-2; 7 (The Living Bible)

Can you just enjoy and delight in the fact that God wants to do amazing things through you for his glory? Can you stop worrying just for a minute about having to produce your own happiness and fulfillment?

RADICAL TRUTH

> "Now glory be to God who by his mighty power at work within us is able to do far more than we would ever dare to ask or even dream of—infinitely beyond our highest prayers, desires, thoughts or hopes."
>
> Ephesians 3:20 (The Living Bible)

Can you give up trying to do everything yourself and instead let God work his will in your life as you keep on doing the right things? How?

Can you commit to do the small, good, right things God asks you to do minute by minute, and then let him take care of the big huge rest of your life? Can you try your best to put God's little daily principles into practice and forget for awhile about getting certain results or outcomes? *Make a list of five little things you can do in the next five minutes that are a response to something God has told you to do.*

A RADICAL Tip

How about including on your list: "Don't be afraid" (decide to replace fear with trust for just this minute). Then try "pray for others" (pray for your children). Then try something like "Be kind" (let someone in front of you in line). Put together an hour of obeying God. Put together a day of doing your best to obey God. See how you feel.

Below, write a letter to God. Be honest. You don't have to be thankful for the situation you are in, but try being thankful for the good things God can bring out of it. Tell God what you are afraid of. Tell God that you need his help continually. Tell him that you want his purposes fulfilled in you. Tell him that, even though you cannot see it now, you will believe his promises to give you the desires of your heart. God knows your heart anyway, so don't sugarcoat what you say to him. Do this every morning for a week. For this one week, commit to trusting God even though your life seems to be a mess.

RADICAL TRUTH

> **REMEMBER THIS—**
>
> " ... with God, everything is possible."
>
> Matthew 19:26b (The Living Bible)
>
>

Discuss any unresolved issues from the Embrace Transformation chapter in *Radical Recovery*.

Week Ten

Conclusion—Or New Beginning— However You Look At It!

RADICAL TRUTH

> "Trust in the Lord and do good;
>   dwell in the land and enjoy safe pasture.
> Delight yourself in the Lord
>   and he will give you the desires of your heart.
> Commit your way to the Lord;
>   trust in him and he will do this:
> He will make your righteousness shine like the dawn,
>   the justice of your cause like the noonday sun.
> Be still before the Lord and wait patiently for him;
>   do not fret when men succeed in their ways,
>   when they carry out their wicked schemes.
> Refrain from anger and turn from wrath;
>   do not fret—it only leads to evil.
> For evil men will be cut off,
>   but those who hope in the Lord
>   will inherit the land."
>
> Psalm 37:3-9 (NIV)

What are some of the important lessons you have learned throughout this study?
List below.

Are you getting to a more optimistic, God-based view of your future? *Explain.*

Write below ten "power" words that describe you now. Examples: "confident, peaceful, strong, healthy, focused, enthusiastic …"

RADICAL TRUTH

> "What a wonderful God we have—he is the Father of our Lord Jesus Christ, the source of every mercy, and the one who so wonderfully comforts and strengthens us in our hardships and trials. And why does he do this? So that when others are troubled, needing our sympathy and encouragement, we can pass on to them this same help and comfort God has given us."
>
> 2 Corinthians 1:3-4 (The Living Bible)

RADICAL TRUTH

> "Strength is for service, not status. Each one of us needs to look after the good of those around us, asking 'How can I help?'"
>
> Romans 15:2 (The Message)

Watch for people who need your encouragement. Because of what you have been going through, you can better understand what people need when they are suffering. God has comforted and blessed you so that you can bless others. Your suffering gives you great opportunity to serve. Can you think of anyone right now who needs your particular encouragement? Write the person's name here and pray for them and then look for ways to ease their pain. This is part of God's plan for you.

Discuss any issues that are still unresolved for you.

Plan to get together as a group in about a month to see how everyone is doing. Stay in touch with each other. Support each other. Get together individually. Pass along or suggest the *www.midlifedivorcerecovery.com* website or the book or workbook to someone else who might need it.

Please send me any suggestions or recommendations to improve or add to this study.

Contact me if you would be interested in helping put together a one-day Divorce Recovery Bootcamp or seminar or support group in your area.

For more information go to: *www.midlifedivorcerecovery.com*.

Contact:
Suzy Brown
suzysuccess@kc.rr.com

Or call:
816-941-4911
913-558-5312 (cell)

Notes